Sad

Julie Murray

Abdo
EMOTIONS
Kids

abdopublishing.com

Published by Abdo Kids, a division of ABDO, PO Box 398166, Minneapolis, Minnesota 55439.
Copyright © 2017 by Abdo Consulting Group, Inc. International copyrights reserved in all countries.
No part of this book may be reproduced in any form without written permission from the publisher.

Printed in the United States of America, North Mankato, Minnesota.

052016

092016

 THIS BOOK CONTAINS
RECYCLED MATERIALS

Photo Credits: iStock, Shutterstock

Production Contributors: Teddy Borth, Jennie Forsberg, Grace Hansen

Design Contributors: Candice Keimig, Dorothy Toth

Cataloging-in-Publication Data

Names: Murray, Julie, author.

Title: Sad / by Julie Murray.

Description: Minneapolis, MN : Abdo Kids, [2017] | Series: Emotions | Includes
    bibliographical references and index.

Identifiers: LCCN 2015959120 | ISBN 9781680805253 (lib. bdg.) |
    ISBN 9781680805819 (ebook) | ISBN 9781680806373 (Read-to-me ebook)

Subjects: LCSH: Sadness--Juvenile literature. | Emotions--Juvenile literature.

Classification: DDC 152.4--dc23

LC record available at http://lccn.loc.gov/2015959120

Table of Contents

Sad

We feel unhappy when we are sad. It is an **emotion**.

Laura feels bullied.

She is sad.

We feel sad when we miss someone. Erin misses her dad.

We feel sad when we are sick.

James is in the hospital.

Luke lost the game.

He feels sad.

Megan's feelings are hurt.

She feels sad.

15

Jake fights with his friend.

He feels sad.

Kate feels left out.

She feels sad.

19

What makes you feel sad?

21

Things to Do When We Are Sad

listen to a favorite song

take a long walk outside

read a good book

talk to a parent or
friend about it

Glossary

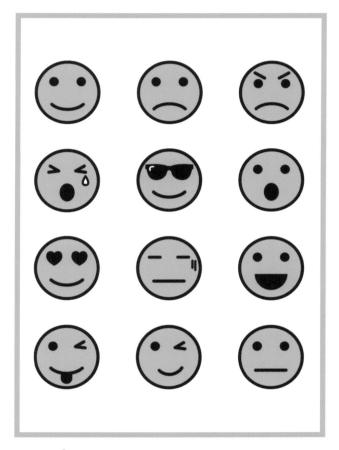

emotion
a strong feeling.

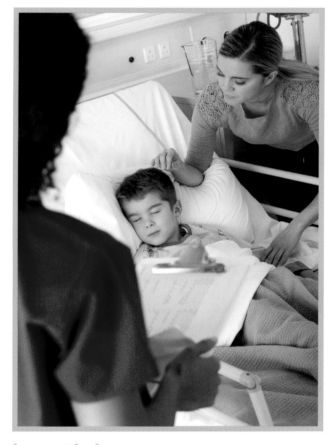

hospital
a place where people go to get help
if they are sick or hurt.

Index

abdokids.com

Use this code to log on to abdokids.com and access crafts, games, videos, and more!

Abdo Kids Code:
ESK5253